Gathering in Prayer
Words for Inclusive Worship

Roger Courtney

The Lindsey Press
London

Published by the Lindsey Press
on behalf of the General Assembly of Unitarian
and Free Christian Churches
Essex Hall, 1–6 Essex Street, London WC2R 3HY, UK

© The General Assembly of Unitarian and Free Christian Churches, 2010

ISBN 978-0-85319-081-3

Designed and typeset by Garth Stewart, Oxford

Printed and bound in the United Kingdom by
Lightning Source, Milton Keynes

CONTENTS

Introduction

What follows is a collection of prayers which reflect the need for original, intelligent and inclusive public worship material, dealing with the real challenges of living a life of faith in the 21st Century.

Although written essentially from within the Christian tradition, many of the prayers are also suitable for use in interfaith services and gatherings. Some are specifically inspired by sayings and sacred writings from other traditions.

It feels as though there is something very strange going on when someone from a low non-liturgical church background starts writing prayers and meditations based on the process of a liturgy. But perhaps it is precisely because I come from a church background that does not value liturgy that, as I have experienced it in inter-denominational services, I have increasingly begun to appreciate its beauty, value and ability to inspire and create a real sense of shared community, even amongst those with very diverse beliefs.

Roman Catholic, Anglican and Orthodox churches already have their own liturgies, many of which are very old and very beautiful. This is not an attempt to try and replace them, but to provide a source of prayers and meditations, particularly for inter-denominational, non-denominational, and interfaith services and gatherings where it would be appropriate to share common aspects of an inclusive vision and values based on a faith perspective.

These prayers are organised under themed headings. They are designed to be used selectively and flexibly, complementing other aspects of worship.

Roger Courtney

Gathering

Welcome

Those who seek a deeper understanding of their faith

> – *We bid you welcome*

Those who come seeking forgiveness and healing

> – *We bid you welcome*

Those who seek silence for reflection, meditation or prayer

> – *We bid you welcome*

Those who share a commitment to love, justice, truth and beauty

> – *We bid you welcome*

These who seek the divine presence

> – *We bid you welcome*

Those who feel lonely and seek company, or those who just want to get out of the rain

> – *We bid you welcome*

Whoever you are and whyever you came

> – *We bid you welcome*

A very warm welcome to all of you

Gathering Together

In this fragmented world
- *We gather together in search of wholeness*

In this world full of conflict
- *We gather together in search of peace*

In this world full of injustice and oppression
- *We gather together in search of justice*

In this world full of deceit and ignorance
- *We gather together in search of truth*

In this world full of brutality and ugliness
- *We gather together in search of beauty*

In this world full of loneliness
- *We gather together in search of love*

In this world full of superficiality and commercialism
- *We gather together in search of meaning and the divine presence in our lives*

This Place

In a world full of violence
- *May this be a place of peacemaking*

In a world full of conflict
- *May this be a place of reconciliation*

In a world full of lies and ignorance
- *May this be a place of truth-seeking*

In a world full of fragmentation
- *May this be a place of wholeness*

In a world full of cynicism and doubt
- *May this be a place of hope and celebration*

In a world full of materialism
- *May this be a place of spirit*

Welcome into the Circle

In a world full of bitterness and fear
  - *Welcome into the circle of unconditional love*

In a world where so many people face injustice and oppression
  - *Welcome into the circle of fairness and freedom*

In a world full of lies and misinformation
  - *Welcome into the circle of openness and truth*

In a world full of guilt and remorse
  - *Welcome into the circle of forgiveness*

In a world full of materialism and selfishness
  - *Welcome into the circle of service to others*

In a world full of conflict and bitterness
  - *Welcome into the circle of reconciliation and peace*

Come and Experience

All of those whose lives feel empty or meaningless

- *Come and experience the possibility of meaning and the healing of the spirit*

All of those who have had their heart broken

- *Come and experience the possibility of healing of the heart*

All of those who feel cynical or pessimistic

- *Come and experience the possibility of hope for the future*

All of those whose lives are filled with superficiality

- *Come and experience the possibility of stimulation for the mind and the soul*

All of those whose lives are filled with noise

- *Come and experience the possibility of silence and tranquillity to reconnect with who we are and the divine ground of all things*

Take Time

As we prepare ourselves for worship
Let us take time just to be quiet

> *(pause)*

Let us take time to take breath and let the worries of the
week slip away

> *(pause)*

Let us take time to give thanks for all the good things in our
lives

> *(pause)*

Let us take time to think about those who can't be with us

> *(pause)*

Let us take time to pray for those who need help

> *(pause)*

Let us take time to reflect on our own lives and what we
need to do to live up to our highest ideals

Commitment

Asking for Forgiveness

We confess the harm that has been done in the name of religion and ask for forgiveness.

When religion has been used to justify war and other forms of violence

– *We ask for forgiveness*

When religion has been used to make ourselves feel superior to others whose beliefs are different

– *We ask for forgiveness*

When religion has been used to exercise power over others or promote our own society's interests

– *We ask for forgiveness*

When religion has been used to create or reinforce division and conflict

– *We ask for forgiveness*

When religion has been used to judge and condemn others for their beliefs

– *We ask for forgiveness*

When religion has been used to discriminate against people because of their gender or sexuality

– *We ask for forgiveness*

When religion has been used to trample on other cultures

   – *We ask for forgiveness*

Guide us each day towards a faith based on unconditional selfless love and a humble search for truth and justice

Focusing on what is Important

In a world where the majority of the world's population lives on less than £1 a day

    – Help us to focus our attention on what is most important

In a world where every three seconds someone dies needlessly of malnutrition or preventable disease

    – Help us to focus our attention on what is most important

In a world where tens of thousands of species become extinct every year, rapidly reducing the biodiversity of the planet

    – Help us to focus our attention on what is most important

In a world where over only a couple of centuries we have used up nearly all the natural resources on the earth accumulated over tens of millions of years

    – Help us to focus our attention on what is most important

In a world where the carbon emissions of the rich world threaten to irreversibly alter global climate patterns with potentially disastrous results for the whole world

    – Help us to focus our attention on what is most important

In a world where the last century saw two world wars, numerous genocides and the use and proliferation of nuclear weapons, increasing the likelihood that this century will be our last

    – Help us to focus our attention on what is most important

In a world where millions of people live under brutal
military dictatorships, denied even basic human rights

   – Help us to focus our attention on what is most important

In a world where the enormity of the problems facing the
human race threaten to overwhelm us, or where we easily
become distracted with irrelevant activities and concerns

   – Help us to focus our attention on what is most important

In a world where even simple actions can make a real
difference to the lives of others and help create a positive
future for millions of people

   – Help us to focus our attention on what is most important

Let Justice Flow

When religious orthodoxy becomes more important than the needs of the poorest in society

- *Let justice flow like water, and integrity like an ever-flowing stream*

When our desire for a peaceful and comfortable life leads us to exclude others

- *Let justice flow like water, and integrity like an ever-flowing stream*

When inequality of wealth and power means that many go without basic resources to live, and others are excluded from mainstream society

- *Let justice flow like water, and integrity like an ever-flowing stream*

When people are marginalized and devalued because of their age or disability; or because of their religious or political views or background

- *Let justice flow like water, and integrity like an ever-flowing stream*

When the churches are more concerned with maintaining their institutions and buildings than their responsibility to the poor

- *Let justice flow like water, and integrity like an ever-flowing stream*

Commitment to Social Change

In a world full of injustice

- *we commit ourselves to work for justice*

In a world full of violence

- *we commit ourselves to work for peace*

In a world full of poverty

- *we commit ourselves to work for the development of the poorest communities*

In a world full of inequality

- *we commit ourselves to work for equality*

In a world full of fear and conflict

- *we commit ourselves to work for reconciliation*

In a world full of discrimination

- *we commit ourselves to work for human rights*

In a world full of spiritual emptiness

- *we commit ourselves to help others find meaning in their lives and to work for the expansion of the Kingdom of God through love*

Conquer
(inspired by a Buddhist saying)

When so much of the world seems to be filled with bitterness and hate

- *Help us to conquer anger with love*

When those with power so often act unjustly, destroying lives in the process

- *Help us to conquer evil with good*

When greed and consumerism seem to dominate the world

- *Help us to conquer selfishness with generosity*

When facts are so often distorted at the expense of others

- *Help us to conquer lies with the truth*

The Way

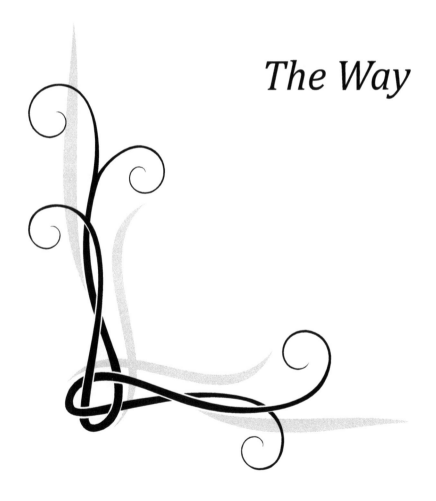

Jesus Asks Us

In showing unconditional love for others without concern for ourselves

> – *Jesus asks us to follow him*

In accepting and valuing others, without judgement or condemnation

> – *Jesus asks us to follow him*

In loving our enemies and those most despised by society

> – *Jesus asks us to follow him*

In visiting those who are sick or in prison

> – *Jesus asks us to follow him*

In helping the poor and powerless, living next door or on the other side of the city or the planet

> – *Jesus asks us to follow him*

In standing up for what is right, regardless of the consequences

> – *Jesus asks us to follow him*

In forgiving those who have wronged us, or those close to us

> – *Jesus asks us to follow him*

In living life in all its fullness and enabling others to do the same

> – *Jesus asks us to follow him*

In healing damaged lives and damaged relationships

> – *Jesus asks us to follow him*

Help Us

In our daily lives help us to be more like Jesus

When we become aware of people who are in need
- *Help us to care like him*

When we are tempted to jealously and selfishly protect our possessions
- *Help us to share like him*

When our ears are deaf to the needs and stories of others
- *Help us to hear like him*

When we are tempted to remain silent because we might face criticism if we spoke up
- *Help us to face fear like him*

When we are tempted to think that we already know it all
- *Help us to seek the truth like him*

When we are tempted to be economical with the truth for our own gain
- *Help us to speak the truth like him*

When we are blinded by bitterness or prejudice
- *Help us to see like him*

continued overleaf

In all our thoughts and actions, regardless of the challenges
life throws at us
- *Help us to be like him*

In trying to live up to our highest ideals
- *Help us to be the best that we can be*

Unconditional Love

We celebrate self-giving unconditional love.

Love that: has no expectations

seeks no reward

requires no gratitude

experiences no fear or bitterness

and is only concerned about the wellbeing of others

Not to Judge

When we feel tempted to make assumptions about other people because of their background or affiliation

- *Help us not to judge other people*

When we disagree with someone's point of view

- *Help us not to judge other people*

When we are tempted to look down on someone else's ideas because they are unorthodox, heretical, irrational, or old-fashioned

- *Help us not to judge other people*

When we see someone make a mistake

- *Help us not to judge other people*

When we feel our own position is more logical, sensible or important than others

- *Help us not to judge other people*

When we are tempted to exclude or devalue others because of things they have said or done

- *Help us not to judge other people*

Who is our Neighbour?

- *We recognise and value those who have religious or political beliefs that are different from us*

- *We recognise and value those who are a different nationality or race from us*

- *We recognise and value those who experience poverty and hardship*

- *We recognise and value those who are disabled by society*

- *We recognise and value those who live with the daily challenge of mental health problems or addiction*

- *We recognise and value those who have been the victims of violence*

- *We recognise and value those who have experienced the loss of a loved one*

- *We recognise and value those who are struggling with doubt or despair*

- *We recognise and value those who face problems of illness and poor health*

- *We recognise and value those who are in prison*

- *We recognise and value all those who feel excluded from the love and concern of others*

- *We recognise and celebrate the divine forgiveness and love that is available for the asking*

The Life of Faith

True Faith

True faith cannot be found by taking part in religious rituals

True faith cannot be found by reading sacred books

True faith cannot be found by reciting creeds, prayers or mantras

True faith can only be found by living it

True faith can only be known by becoming faith-full.

Truth and Doubt

We were probably all brought up with the idea that to believe
was good and to doubt was bad,
so when we experience doubt, as everyone does, we feel guilty.
And so, we keep our doubts to ourselves.
It took a long time for me to realise that truth and doubt are
the two sides of the one coin. All the great leaps forward
in human knowledge are because someone doubted what
was being handed down as received wisdom.
What if the sun doesn't go round the earth, but it's the other
way round?
What if the world isn't flat, but round?
What if the world wasn't actually made in 40 days, but life has
evolved by natural selection over millions of years?
The pioneers who first expressed these doubts usually
suffered badly for contradicting the official wisdom,
so coming to those new truths required great courage.
But it first of all required doubt, a scepticism about received
wisdom.
So we should never be ashamed to experience and express our
doubts about received wisdom, including religious beliefs.
Only by experiencing and sharing these doubts can we come
to new and deeper truths.
Faith does not come out of certainty, but out of doubt.

Truthfulness

When we are tempted to lie for our own benefit

- *Let our conduct be marked by truthfulness in thought,
word and deed*

When we are tempted to be economical with the truth, by
failing to say what we should

- *Let our conduct be marked by truthfulness in thought,
word and deed*

When we don't listen to someone else's truth

- *Let our conduct be marked by truthfulness in thought,
word and deed*

When we want to distort the facts to suit ourselves

- *Let our conduct be marked by truthfulness in thought,
word and deed*

When we stop being open to the possibility of being wrong

- *Let our conduct be marked by truthfulness in thought,
word and deed*

Belief

When I can't see the presence of God in a selfish world
- *Help my unbelief*

When I can't see the impact of being loving
- *Help my unbelief*

When I begin to doubt my faith
- *Help my unbelief*

When I begin to believe that being selfish might get me the things I want in life
- *Help my unbelief*

When I am tempted to stay silent rather than challenge those who are hurting others
- *Help my unbelief*

When I am tempted to devalue others
- *Help my unbelief*

When I am not sure what the purpose of it all is
- *Help my unbelief*

I believe
- *Help my unbelief*

Help Us To Pray

Prayer is the opportunity:

To honestly reflect on our lives
- *Help us to pray*

To contemplate our deepest values and concerns
- *Help us to pray*

To be still and listen to the person we really are and the divine spirit within us
- *Help us to pray*

To access the pool of renewal, healing and forgiveness, which is always available to us
- *Help us to pray*

To gain the courage to step beyond the security boundaries that surround us and love unconditionally
- *Help us to pray*

To give thanks for the wondrous gifts we have been given
- *Help us to pray*

To share our hopes and concerns with other seekers of the truth
- *Help us to pray*

To be silent and empty our minds of all thought and concerns and allow ourselves to be filled with love and joy

    – *Help us to pray*

To let the spirit of God flow through us

    – *Help us to pray*

When I Pray
(inspired by Rabindrath Tagore)

Let me not pray to have my doubts vanish

> But that I have courage to follow my doubts where they take me in pursuit of truth.

Let me not pray that I never again experience the loss of a loved one

> But that I have the strength to both honour the memory and bring comfort to others.

Let me not pray that my faith is not challenged

> But that my anger is clothed in love and directed at injustice and oppression.

Let me not pray that I won't face cruelty or violence

> But that I don't allow the experience to turn me into a victim motivated by bitterness.

Let me not pray for wealth and comfort

> But that I have the commitment to work ceaselessly for those who are poor and powerless.

Let me not pray to have infinite knowledge and wisdom

> But for the humility to recognise the limitations of what I know and value the truth and wisdom in others.

Let me not pray for eternal life

> But to live this life well and to help others to do the same.

Hope

Hope is not blind optimism – it is where expectation and commitment meet

We celebrate hope:

- *that good will conquer evil*

- *that unconditional love is the most powerful force, which can truly change the world*

- *that forgiveness is available to each of us, to free us from the guilt of the past*

- *that each of us is loved and valued*

- *that we will achieve hope in our own lives, by bringing hope to others*

Courage

Divine spirit, in the face of pressure, even ridicule, from others, grant us the courage

- *to express our own beliefs and doubts*

- *to be fully and authentically ourselves*

- *to value those who have been devalued*

- *to speak up for those who are poor and powerless*

- *to challenge systems that maintain people in powerlessness and poverty*

- *to stand up to our fears, and pressure from others*

- *not to give in to bitterness and resentment*

- *not to strike back, or seek revenge*

but to follow the path of courage, wherever it might lead

Silence

Today it is hard to find silence
We are bombarded by noise from all sides
And when we might be able to find silence
We destroy it by turning on some noise
In order to find distraction from ourselves
Because we are restless
Uncomfortable in our own skins.

If we experience the stillness of silence
We might have to look deep inside ourselves
And we are not sure if we would like what we would find.

Mother Teresa said "God is the friend of silence"
The trees, plants and flowers all grow in silence
The sun, moon and stars all move in silence.

Let us take a few moments to enjoy silence
To allow ourselves to be who we are
To be comfortable with who we are
To allow the divine to flow through us

In the Silence

As George Fox, the founder of the Society of Friends, also
known as the Quakers, and the many mystics down the ages
understood well, worship is not simply for public display of
our faith in certain creeds or dogmas, or to ask for things in
prayer, but the opportunity to take time out from our daily
lives,

- *to re-connect with the source of all life and all love*

- *to be refreshed and renewed*

- *to listen to the divine spirit that permeates all things*

- *to seek the healing of broken bodies, broken lives, broken
relationships*

- *to seek forgiveness for the things we have done wrong*

- *to reflect on the deepest meaning of our lives*

- *to recommit to try and follow the right way*

In the silence that follows, let the divine spirit fill our hearts.

Human Gifts

Unique Awareness

Of all living beings, we alone have an awareness of our own existence, our potential, our impact on others, and our mortality.

With this unique awareness comes a unique responsibility:

- *to live to our potential*

- *to be aware of our impact on others, and*

- *to leave the world better than we found it*

Talents

We commit ourselves:

- *To use whatever talents we have to increase the amount of love, beauty, truth and justice in the world.*

- *To help others to identify their unique talents and help them to develop and grow.*

- *To work to remove the barriers that prevent individuals and groups recognising and using their distinctive abilities.*

- *To celebrate the example of Jesus, who broke social taboos and barriers to show respect for other people, particularly those that society tended to despise.*

- *To appreciate and celebrate the gifts in others.*

Work and Human Dignity

We acknowledge the need to work to support ourselves and our dependants and to promote human dignity.

We celebrate those who love the work they do and whose work is valuable to society.

We celebrate the value of work that is unwaged because it is carried out within the family, like bringing up children or managing a household.

We also celebrate the opportunity to do gift-work outside of the family – voluntary work that benefits the community and through which we can grow and develop.

We pray for those who are unemployed, or in employment that is oppressive or unfulfilling.

We acknowledge times when we have made choices in work for the benefit of ourselves, at the expense of others.

We commit ourselves to find ways to use work (paid and unpaid) to use our distinctive talents and to contribute to beauty, truth, wisdom, justice, happiness or peace in the world.

Development of Others
(Inspired by a Jain saying)

To love is to work to remove the barriers that prevent others
developing and achieving their potential. Let us reflect on
the lives of those who are most restricted by our attitudes
and thoughtlessness.

For those who have literacy or numeracy problems

- *No obstacle should be created in the development of
  others*

For those that other people say are too old, or too young

- *No obstacle should be created in the development of
  others*

For those with a physical or sensory disability

- *No obstacle should be created in the development of
  others*

For those with learning difficulties or mental health
problems

- *No obstacle should be created in the development of
  others*

For those discriminated against because of their beliefs or
background

- *No obstacle should be created in the development of
  others*

Learning

We acknowledge our debt to so many people who have gone before us: those who have shared something of the joy of their learning journey with us.

> – *We celebrate their contribution towards truth and wisdom in the world.*

We acknowledge that learning requires a sceptical and enquiring mind.

> – *We celebrate those who have swum against the tide to bring us new insights and new questions.*

We acknowledge that many people have had a bad experience of formal education, leading them to believe they are failures and that learning is not for them.

> – *We celebrate those who work with people who have had a negative experience of education, to help them recover the joy of learning.*

We acknowledge that the purposes of education are to encourage an enquiring mind, instil a love of learning, and create a passion for particular subjects.

> – *We celebrate those special individuals who have inspired our passion for learning.*

We acknowledge that our own development and that of society depends on our continued commitment to learning.

> – *We celebrate the opportunities that exist for us to pursue truth and wisdom.*

Children

"Whosoever welcomes the littlest of these children welcomes me."
Jesus put children at the heart of his vision of the kingdom of heaven, but our society so often fails them

- *Jesus said that the kingdom of heaven belongs to little children*

Children are often left to feel they are inadequate failures

- *Jesus said that the kingdom of heaven belongs to little children*

Children are often told by adults that they should be seen but not heard

- *Jesus said that the kingdom of heaven belongs to little children*

Children often suffer because of a lack of love or of loving boundaries

- *Jesus said that the kingdom of heaven belongs to little children*

Many children are abused by adults they trusted, and we fail to protect them

- *Jesus said that the kingdom of heaven belongs to children*

continued overleaf

43

So many children around the world live in abject poverty
  – *Jesus said that the kingdom of heaven belongs to children*

Help us to put children at the heart of our lives and our vision of the future
  – *Jesus said that the kingdom of heaven belongs to children*

Becoming Like Children

Jesus said that we should become like children, so let us commit ourselves:

- *to love others more naturally*

- *to celebrate life more spontaneously*

- *to explore life more inquisitively*

- *to live life more trustingly*

- *to be ourselves more freely and openly*

Children of God

(Based on a speech by Nelson Mandela)

Our deepest fear is not that we are inadequate.
Our deepest fear is that we are all-powerful
beyond measure.

> – *We are all children of God*

It is our light not our darkness that most frightens us.
We ask ourselves: Who am I to be brilliant, gorgeous,
talented, fabulous?
Actually, who am I not to be?

> – *We are all children of God*

Our playing small does not serve the world.
There is nothing enlightening about shrinking,
so that other people won't feel insecure around us.

> – *We are all children of God*

We are meant to shine as children do.
We were born to make manifest the glory of God that is
within us;
it's in everyone.

> – *We are all children of God*

And as we let our light shine
we unconsciously give other people permission to do the
same.
As we are liberated from our own fear,
our presence automatically liberates others.

> – *We are all children of God*

Families

We give thanks for families of all shapes and sizes, which provide such an important basis for love and support in our society.

We give thanks for the joy and wonder of children, whom Jesus said we should strive to be like, and from whom we have so much to learn.

We give thanks for parents who give so much of themselves to ensure that children feel loved and valued.

We give thanks, too, for grandparents and other family members, who so often share the responsibilities of parenting and in return are able to share in its joys.

We pray for families that are struggling to cope with the pressures they face: may they find courage and the support they need.

We pray for those who feel damaged or excluded from family life: may they feel the hand of friendship and love and feel included and supported as a family member.

We pray for those who work with and support children and parents: may they in turn find support and encouragement.

continued overleaf

We forgive family members who we feel have let us down, have not lived up to our expectations, or have hurt us. We will continue to love and pray for them unconditionally.

We acknowledge the shortcomings in our own family life and renew our commitment to self-giving love that enables both children and adults to feel cherished and supported.

We pray for support and guidance in helping us to be better family members.

Gender

Our identity as men and women, boys and girls is a very important part of who we are and one that we should celebrate in a spirit of respect and equality.

We acknowledge the times when we have allowed a stereotyped view of men and women to prejudge who someone really is.

- *We celebrate our identity as women or men, girls or boys as something to be enjoyed in a spirit of respect and equality.*

We acknowledge the failings of society to ensure equality between men and women.

- *We celebrate those who have worked to create greater equality and understanding between men and women.*

We acknowledge the shortcomings of the churches in ensuring equality between men and women, and affirm that women can play a full and equal role at all levels in the church.

- *We celebrate those who have challenged traditional forms of theology and church rules and structures that deny the equality of men and women.*

We acknowledge that many people struggle with issues of gender and that struggle is made much worse by the prejudices of other people

- *We celebrate the right to express our own identity in a spirit of love and respect.*
- *We commit ourselves to promoting the equality of men and women in society, regardless of gender, in the churches and in our own lives.*

Always with Us

Those who cared for, nurtured and protected us
- *They are always with us*

Those who have loved us unselfishly
- *They are always with us*

Those we have loved deeply
- *They are always with us*

Those who have inspired us to greater things
- *They are always with us*

Those who have listened to us when we were struggling and helped to guide us on the right track
- *They are always with us*

Those who shared their wisdom with us and enabled us to see more of the truth
- *They are always with us*

Those to whom we have had to say goodbye with great sadness
- *They are always with us*

Valued

Don't let yourself feel devalued by others
   – *Remember, even the hairs on your head are counted*

When you feel people are looking down on you
   – *Remember, even the hairs on your head are counted*

When people don't even seem to notice you exist
   – *Remember, even the hairs on your head are counted*

When you are tempted to stop caring what happens to you
   – *Remember, even the hairs on your head are counted*

Thanksgiving

For the Beauty of the World

On this day we celebrate and give thanks for beauty.

When we look at the smile on the face of a young child, or at flowers in full bloom
- *We give thanks for the beauty of the world*

When we look at an ancient tree in all its glory, or at a stream effortlessly flowing down a mountainside
- *We give thanks for the beauty of the world*

When we watch the waves rolling on to the beach, or look at an inspiring painting or sculpture
- *We give thanks for the beauty of the world*

When we listen to a moving piece of music, or see an inspirational play or dance
- *We give thanks for the beauty of the world*

When we allow our own natural creativity to find expression and when we allow ourselves to feel at one with creation
- *We give thanks for the beauty of the world*

When we realise the importance of beauty in living life in all its fullness
- *We give thanks for the beauty of the world*

Today, we commit ourselves to promote and protect beauty and creativity in all aspects of life for everyone.

With all our Hearts

We recognise that life is a gift and a joy to be lived in all its richness.

- *We give thanks with all our hearts*

We recognise the incredible beauty of the earth.

- *We give thanks with all our hearts*

We recognise that the world has all the resources it needs for all its people to live a fulfilling life.

- *We give thanks with all our hearts*

We recognise that we have been given the understanding and opportunity to create a world where the resources of the world are shared fairly.

- *We give thanks with all our hearts*

We recognise that we have only borrowed this world from our children, and it can provide for future generations if we stop selfishly plundering and damaging its abundant resources.

- *We give thanks with all our hearts*

We recognise that we are lucky enough to share this planet with a wonderful and diverse array of other living beings who are entitled to lives of dignity and fulfilment.

- *We give thanks with all our hearts*

Flowers

Let us give thanks for the beauty of flowers, plants and trees. They teach us some important lessons about life, if we are prepared to listen.

Life is extra-ordinarily beautiful. Even a single flower can fill us with wonder, joy and thanksgiving.

Life is extra-ordinarily diverse – every flower is different. Its shape is different; its colour is different; its smell is different. Part of the beauty is in the diversity.

Flowers naturally blossom and display their radiant glory. We too naturally blossom as human beings if we follow our inner-directed destiny.

Life needs the right external conditions to flourish. Flowers need the right soil and enough water and sunshine to grow and bloom successfully. We too need to ensure that other human beings have the resources and love to flourish as unique human beings.

Flowers need go-betweens like butterflies on the wind to spread the pollen and help the species of flower to grow and expand. We too are called to help build bridges between people and help spread the pollen of peace and reconciliation.

We celebrate and give thanks for the joy and beauty of flowers, plants and trees that can heal and renew us and teach us so much about ourselves and the incredible world we live in.

Continuous Blessing

Life is an original and continuous blessing to be enjoyed, shared and celebrated.

For the beauty of the universe
- *We give thanks and praise*

For the joy of new life in the world
- *We give thanks and praise*

For the beauty and fragrance of a flower in blossom
- *We give thanks and praise*

For the joy of friendship
- *We give thanks and praise*

For the cleansing and refreshing joy of water, pure and simple
- *We give thanks and praise*

For the richness of the diversity of cultures across the globe
- *We give thanks and praise*

For a faith in the power of unconditional love
- *We give thanks and praise*

Celebrate Life

Let us celebrate life – right now!
Let us bask in the sunlight
Let us swim in the cold waters
Let us lie on the grass and look at the sky
Let us close our eyes and revel in all the sounds of nature
Let us smell the joyous perfume of flowers
Let us sit beneath the branches of an ancient tree
Let us meditate on the beauty of a single flower in full bloom
Let us share in the laughter of children
Let us feel the love of those who really care about us
Let us enjoy the knowledge that we have played a part in
enabling others to flourish
Let us give thanks for the astonishing unlikely privilege of
being fully alive in this place and at this time
Let us celebrate God's evolving creation

All Life Is Connected
(inspired by Chief Seattle)

No matter how different someone is from us, they are part of the human family, one of God's children to be valued and treated with dignity.

    – *All of life is connected in an interdependent web*

We need to realise that the earth does not belong to us, but we belong to the earth.

    – *All of life is connected in an interdependent web*

When we ignore the oneness of life and treat the environment as a disposable commodity, we reap the consequences.

    – *All of life is connected in an interdependent web*

Animals have the right to live natural lives without pain and cruelty inflicted by human beings.

    – *All of life is connected in an interdependent web*

When we use up the earth's natural resources we selfishly pass on a damaged and depleted world to our children and grandchildren.

    – *All of life is connected in an interdependent web*

continued overleaf

When we pump chemicals into the air and sea without a thought for the consequences, we threaten the whole future of life on the planet.

    – *All of life is connected in an interdependent web*

Help us to celebrate the oneness of all creation and to live our lives in the knowledge that

    – *All of life is connected in an interdependent web*

Affirmation

We affirm together:

The radiant joy and beauty of the world in which we live

The unity of all life and our interdependence with the rest of creation

Our responsibility to care for and sustain all forms of life on the planet for future generations

The uniqueness and equal dignity of every person

The power of unconditional love to transform lives

The importance of constantly seeking truth and wisdom

Our commitment to support each other in the task of building the Kingdom of Heaven, based on peace, justice and love

The divine ground of our being that connects us with each other and the infinite and which replenishes and heals us

Peace

How Beautiful

When people fearlessly and non-violently stand up against injustice

- *How beautiful on the mountains are the feet of those who bring peace*

When people mediate disputes and act as bridge-builders

- *How beautiful on the mountains are the feet of those who bring peace*

When people are prepared to respect the views and beliefs of those who are very different

- *How beautiful on the mountains are the feet of those who bring peace*

When people are prepared to speak their truth and listen to other people's truths

- *How beautiful on the mountains are the feet of those who bring peace*

When people apologise for past wrong-doings and seek forgiveness and restoration of the relationship

- *How beautiful on the mountains are the feet of those who bring peace*

Strive for Peace

As we return to the pressures of the real world, let us turn away from evil and strive for peace with all our hearts.

When we are tempted to stay within our own group and not build relationships with others who are different
- *Let us turn away from evil and strive for peace with all our hearts*

In conflicts in our own lives, families and communities, when we are tempted to demonise others
- *Let us turn away from evil and strive for peace with all our hearts*

When we settle on a comfortable materialism built on the exploitation of others
- *Let us turn away from evil and strive for peace with all our hearts*

When we refuse to forgive others when they have wronged us
- *Let us turn away from evil and strive for peace with all our hearts*

When we fail to speak out against injustice
- *Let us turn away from evil and strive for peace with all our hearts*

Martin Luther King

In the face of injustice and oppression
- *Give us the strength to love, without counting the cost*

In standing up for what we know to be right
- *Give us the strength to love, without counting the cost*

When it would be safer and more beneficial to our personal interests for us to remain silent.
- *Give us the strength to love, without counting the cost*

When we are tempted to seek revenge, or resort to violence
- *Give us the strength to love, without counting the cost*

When the dream of a better future gets clouded by day-to-day concerns
- *Give us the strength to love, without counting the cost*

When we deviate from the path walked by Jesus, which provided a daily inspiration for Martin Luther King
- *Give us the strength to love, without counting the cost*

Leaving Worship

As We Leave

As we leave worship, let us together commit ourselves:

- *to give thanks each day for the abundant gift and beauty of life*

- *to show love and compassion for others*

- *to listen to the stories of others as they share their journey with us*

- *to challenge injustice when we see it*

- *to forgive others when they go astray*

- *to work to heal broken lives and broken relationships*

- *to try to follow Jesus in everything we do*

Sow Bountifully

Give generously
  - *Those who sow bountifully will reap bountifully*

Laugh heartily
  - *Those who sow bountifully will reap bountifully*

Love unconditionally
  - *Those who sow bountifully will reap bountifully*

Serve continuously
  - *Those who sow bountifully will reap bountifully*

Work unceasingly for justice and peace
  - *Those who sow bountifully will reap bountifully*

Lightning Source UK Ltd.
Milton Keynes UK
UKHW021258060420
361394UK00012B/2629